GLOBAL
GOOD
NEWS

GLOBAL GOOD NEWS

Unseen Work *of the* Catholic Church

JOHN L. ALLEN, JR.

Liguori
ONE LIGUORI DRIVE
LIGUORI MO 63057-9999

Imprimi Potest:
Thomas D. Picton, C.Ss.R.
Provincial, Denver Province
The Redemptorists

Published by Liguori Publications
Liguori, Missouri
To order, call 800-325-9521
www.liguori.org

Scripture citations are from the *New Revised Standard Version of
the Bible,* copyright 1989 by the Division of Christian Education
of the National Council of Churches of Christ in the USA. All
rights reserved. Used with permission.

Liguori Publications, a nonprofit corporation, is an apostolate
of the Redemptorists. To learn more about the Redemptorists,
visit Redemptorists.com.

Printed in the United States of America
14 13 12 11 10   5 4 3 2 1
First edition

Introduction

American Catholics these days may understandably feel a bit down in the dumps about the future of their Church. For those taking an honest look around, the case for despair is sometimes depressingly easy to make.

Every time it seems the Catholic Church has turned the corner on the sexual abuse crisis, for example, a new lawsuit is filed or a new set of documents is unearthed, ripping open the wounds anew. The American Church is often badly divided on matters of faith and politics, symbolized by an acrimonious debate in May 2009 over President Barack Obama's commencement address at the University of Notre Dame, which pitted the country's flagship Catholic university against a wide cross-section of our bishops.

Passing on the faith to the next generation is increasingly difficult; a recent Pew Forum study found that for every one new convert to Catholicism in the United States, the Church loses four existing members.

So it goes, through the familiar litany of the Church's woes. It's precisely such moments, however, that invite thoughtful Catholics to stand back, take a deep breath, and resist the tendency to conclude that the sky is falling in.

From a theological point of view, hope is a core Christian virtue. As Pope Benedict XVI reminded us during his April 2008 visit to the United States, we Catholics are called to be a people of hope. Amid the strongest storms and facing the most seemingly impossible challenges, a Christian can never give way to despair, because our faith already tells us how the story ends—and it ends well, in resurrection and new life.

Yet even without that spiritual consolation, a bit of perspective is in order. In truth, if you were to pin up one of those horizontal timelines of more than two thousand years of Church history against a wall, close your eyes, and randomly toss a dart, at whatever point in time that dart happened to fall, Catholics in that era could just as easily have made a case that the ship was about to sink. Think about the era of Saint Augustine, for example, in the fifth century, when the Roman Empire was disintegrating and with it the only world the Catholic Church had ever known. Think about the middle of the fifteenth century, when the Protestant Reformation shattered the religious unity of Europe. Think about the aftermath of the French Revolution, when Napoleon's troops arrested Pope Pius VII and led him off in chains, proclaiming the end of the papacy.

In every one of those moments, the end seemed near. Yet in every one of those moments, new life was actually stirring that would carry the Catholic Church toward bold new frontiers.

The question this small work attempts to answer is the following: For those with eyes to see, where is that new life taking shape in the Catholic Church today? The good news is that there is actually much basis for hope, both in the global Church and right here at home.

Africa

In pockets of both Europe and the United States, the perception is often that this is a period of entropy for the Catholic Church— fewer priests, fewer religious men and women, and aging congregations of the faithful. It can seem like the Church is inexorably sliding toward decay.

Such a perspective, however, fails to take into account the global dimension of Catholicism. Seen in that perspective, the twentieth century was actually the greatest period of missionary expansion in the history of the Church, eclipsing even the Age of Discovery and the evangelization of the so-called "New World" in the sixteenth and seventeenth centuries.

In 1900, the global Catholic population stood at 266 million, with 200 million living in Europe and North America. By 2000, the Catholic total was 1.1 billion, with 720 million in Latin America, Africa, Asia, and points beyond. Just a century ago, barely 25 percent of the world's Catholics lived in the global South. Today that share is 66 percent, and by mid-century it should be 75 percent. This is the most rapid, most profound, most sweeping transformation of Catholic demography in more than 2,000 years of history.

Africa offers the best example of the "evangelical miracle" of the twentieth century.

At the dawn of the twentieth century, there were just 1.9 million Catholics in sub-Saharan Africa. By 2000, the number was 130 million, a staggering growth rate of 6,708 percent. While some of that expansion was demographic, meaning it was related to high birth rates, much of it was also the fruit of apostolic effort. Africa has almost half of all the adult baptisms of Catholics in the world, considered the surest sign of missionary success.

As a result of that momentum, Catholicism in Africa has a dynamic, vital feel, with little of the hand-wringing and sense of gloom and doom that sometimes pervades the Church in the global North. For one thing, the African Church is incredibly young. Roughly 40 percent of the population in sub-Saharan Africa is under fifteen years of age, which means that when you go to Catholic parishes in Africa, kids are often literally hanging from the rafters. You sometimes don't know if you're at a Mass or a daycare center!

Though it's dangerous to generalize about hundreds of millions of people, in very broad strokes, African Catholics tend to be both strongly pro-life (and thus in favor of traditional positions on abortion and homosexuality), while also strongly anti-war and critical of global economic injustices. In the West, the Church's pro-life camp and its peace-and-justice activists often move in separate worlds and sometimes work at cross purposes. Because of their history and their pastoral realities, African Catholics can be less susceptible to efforts to drive a wedge between these two cornerstones of Catholic social teaching.

Given the massive political, economic, and cultural challenges facing Africa, from war and disease to chronic poverty and ecological devastation, there's a spirit of deep social engagement in the African Church. To pluck just one example almost at random, consider the Nyumbani Children of God Relief Institute in Nairobi, Kenya, which provides a home and loving care for almost one hundred HIV/AIDS orphans. ("Nyumbani" means "home" in Swahili.)

Kenya has been among the countries hardest hit by the AIDS crisis, with 2.3 million HIV/AIDS cases between the ages of 15 and 49, according to United Nations statistics, out of a total population of 30 million. More than 1.5 million Kenyan children have been orphaned due to AIDS, and some 300,000 orphans are themselves HIV-positive. HIV-positive orphans are often abandoned by their families, and many have watched their own parents die from AIDS. They wind up being cared for by extended relatives or living on the streets, dropped off at parishes or police stations, and often arrive at state-run orphanages unequipped to deal with their problems.

Nyumbani takes these children in, gives them a traditional African home, provides medical care (including anti-retroviral medications, thereby saving the lives of these children), and makes sure they go to school.

While visiting Nyumbani in 2005, I met John Mwangi, an articulate 14-year-old who had recently been selected to represent Nairobi at a national conference on child and drug abuse. He described the questions he had put to government ministers at the conference with the practiced eloquence of a courtroom attorney. He told me he dreams of going into public affairs, and I could easily imagine him president of Kenya someday. Smiling and joking with Mwangi, one could almost forget that without Nyumbani, this promising young man—and hundreds more like him over the years—would almost certainly be dead. If that's not a story of hope, I'm not quite sure what is.

Of course, Catholicism in Africa has its challenges. During the October 2009 Synod for Africa, more than 200 African bishops were remarkably candid about the Church's failures, admitting that everywhere there is corruption and poor governance in Africa, Catholics are involved, and everywhere there is armed conflict and bloodshed, Catholics are once again complicit in the carnage. All that points to the need for a much more thorough evangelization, because the real measure of missionary success isn't headcounts but rather lives transformed by the Gospel.

Yet despite those challenges, Africa promises to bring massive new energy to the Church in the 21st century. Perhaps most significantly, that energy will be focused largely on changing the world, rather that fighting the stale internal battles that consume so much Catholic energy in the West.

Latin America

From the outside, Latin America might not seem like much of a "good news" story for the Catholic Church. During the late 20th century, a rising tide of Christian Pentecostalism swept across Latin America, eroding once homogenously Catholic societies.

Belgian Passionist Fr. Franz Damen, a veteran staffer for the Bolivian bishops, concluded in the 1990s that conversions from Catholicism to Protestantism in Latin America during the 20th century actually surpassed the Protestant Reformation in Europe in the 16th century. A study commissioned in the late 1990s by CELAM, the Conference of Bishops of Latin America and the Caribbean, found that 8,000 Latin Americans were deserting the Catholic Church every day. A 2005 poll by Latinobarometro, a Chile-based firm that conducts polls in 17 Latin American countries, found that 71 percent of Latin Americans considered themselves Roman Catholic in 2004, down from 80 percent in 1995. If that trend continues at its current pace, the authors speculated, only 50 percent of Latin Americans would identify as Catholics by 2025.

Those losses exposed in dramatic fashion what many analysts had long regarded as the structural weaknesses of Catholicism in Latin America. One is a chronic priest shortage. While Americans may lament the difficulty of generating new vocations, we are still comparatively priest-rich. The priest-to-Catholic ratio in the United States is roughly 1 to 1,300, while in Latin America it's almost 1 to 8,000. Couple that with what historically has been a fairly clerical model of leadership in Latin America, and it's not hard to understand why there are gaping holes in the Church's pastoral network.

Over the centuries, the Church in Latin America also relied, in the eyes of many observers, upon a model of catechesis that didn't always result in the acquisition of an adult faith, leaving many Catholics vulnerable to whatever new wind might blow. In Spanish, there's a saying that captures the frequent reality of the Latin American religious landscape: *Católico ignorante, futuro protestante,* meaning, "An ignorant Catholic is a future Protestant."

A little bit of Economics 101, however, tells us that monopolies tend to become lazy and inefficient, while competition can get the blood pumping. That seems to be exactly what's happening, because while the raw numbers of Catholics may be lower in Latin America today, there's an activist spirit stirring across the continent that's qualitatively new.

During their 2008 assembly in Aparecida, Brazil, the Latin American bishops provided a vocabulary for this new spirit, issuing a bold call for a "Grand Continental Mission."

In his 2008 book, *Conversion of a Continent*, Dominican Fr. Edward Cleary argues that Latin America is in the grip of a religious upheaval, with Pentecostalism as its leading edge. Catholicism, Cleary says, is also becoming more dynamic in Latin America, generating higher levels of commitment among those who remain. Cleary believes that this Catholic awakening had its roots in lay movements that go back to the 1930s and 40s, but it's been jump-started by some healthy competition from the Pentecostals. Clearly argues that despite its statistical losses, Catholicism in Latin America is actually much stronger because of the Pentecostal presence.

Vocations are one measure of this reawakening. In Honduras, the national seminary had an enrollment of 170 in 2007, an all-time high for a country where the total number of priests is slightly more than 400. Twenty years ago, there were fewer than 40 candidates. Bolivia saw the most remarkable increase; in 1972, the entire country had 49 seminarians, while in 2001 the number was 714, representing growth of 1,357 percent. Overall, seminarians in Latin America have gone up 440 percent in the last twenty years, according to statistics collected by the "Religion in Latin America" Web site created by Cleary.

Today, Latin American Catholics seem far more willing to take the missionary bull by the horns. Consider, for example, Franciscan Sr. Maria Rosa Leggol, a feisty octogenarian nun in Honduras, generally described as the "Mother Teresa of Central America." Despite living in a Latin America society, and for that matter a Church long dominated by the ethos of *machismo*, Leggol's story shows that a determined woman can move mountains. Leggol is the founder of the *Sociedad Amigos de los Niños*, which gives abandoned and abused Honduran children a loving home, an education, and prospects for future employment. In the half-century she's been at it, Leggol estimates she's been a "mother and father" to roughly 40,000 such children, many of whom are what she calls "moral orphans"— so badly failed by their own parents as to be effectively without a family.

Or take Maria Luisa Chumpitaz, a Catholic mother of nine, a local legend in an impoverished rural community of 2,000 called "Villa El Carmen," located roughly two hours north of Peru's capital city, Lima. Villa El Carmen was founded in the 1980s by indigenous Peruvians from the Andes Mountains fleeing violence between Maoist-inspired "Shining Path" rebels and the army. Despite the galling poverty of the place— homes without roofs or lights, open sewage, the stench of smoke, serious malnutrition— Chumpitaz, with just two years of primary education, created and ran a women's center widely seen as a regional model for female empowerment. She taught basic literacy skills to rural Andean women, most of them from mountain sites so remote that they'd never even picked up a pencil, let alone written with it. While the women did their writing exercises, Chumpitaz (known locally as "Lucha") and her volunteers fed the children, checked them for disease, and coordinated food pick-ups and drop-offs for the families. Lucha ran the center all the way up to her unexpected death in February 2007.

Perhaps the best example of today's Latin American ferment is the charismatic movement, a high-octane form of praise and worship that in some ways provides a home within the Catholic Church for Pentecostal-style spirituality, including its lively faith in the supernatural—miracles, wonders, healings, revelations, and speaking in tongues.

Oscar Osorio provides one face of today's charismatic wave. An articulate Honduran layman with a wife and four children, Osorio is a star of Channel 48, the Catholic television network in Honduras, where his high-octane, Bible-based preaching opens each morning's programming. Part of Osorio's appeal is that he unabashedly speaks the same deeply personal, spiritual language which has driven the phenomenal growth of Pentecostal Christianity across the globe, especially in Latin America. Osorio laughs that a growing number of Pentecostals attend his retreats, some telling him afterwards: "Great preaching, brother…it's hard to believe you're Catholic!"

Many experts believe that the growing charismatic movement has helped the Catholic Church stem the tide of its losses to the Pentecostals. As a result, a broadly charismatic style is already well on its way to becoming the *de facto* "southern way" of being Catholic. It's also bringing a massive wave of pumped-up, exuberant, explosive energy into the Catholic Church, which usually feels like the spiritual equivalent of Jolt Cola!

What we are seeing today in Latin America is that the Catholic Church's long-slumbering giant seems to be waking up. If a new spirit of missionary outreach and social activism continues to gather force among this bloc of more than 400 million Catholics, the implications for the global Church could be enormous—and enormously hopeful.

The New Faces of the American Church

Some Americans might be tempted at this point to ask, "That's all well and good for Africa or Latin America, but what about here at home?" While understandable, that reaction is based on a faulty ecclesiological premise. The Church in the United States isn't a self-contained reality, hermetically sealed off from the rest of the world; we are part of a global family of faith, and both by design and in fact, our destiny is inevitably bound up with that of our Catholic brothers and sisters elsewhere.

Here's one statistic worth pondering: the roughly 70 million Catholics in America represent six percent of the global Catholic population of 1.2 billion, meaning that 94 percent of the Catholics in the world aren't living in the United States. Any expectation that American interests or preoccupations can or should dominate the global Church is therefore an illusion.

That said, there's also much basis for hope on the domestic front. One source of new life is the rising immigrant tide in the American Church, fueled largely, though not exclusively, by explosive growth in the Hispanic population in the United States.

A recent Pew Forum study of religion in America projects that somewhere around the year 2030, white non-Hispanic Catholics will, for the first time, be a minority within the American Catholic population. Whites will represent 48 percent of the Catholic total, with Hispanics at 41 percent, Asian-Americans at 7.5 percent, and African and African-American Catholics at 3 percent. In fact, the Pew Forum study found that despite the statistic cited above—that American Catholicism loses four members for every one new member it attracts—the Catholic Church is holding steady at one-quarter of the national population, due to the impact of immigration and higher-than-average Hispanic birth rates.

The result is that while the Catholic Church may be struggling in some traditional population centers, above all in the Northeast, it's bursting at the seams in the South and across the Southwest. By mid-century, Texas alone could plausibly have at least six dioceses with a Catholic population in excess of two million: Austin, Brownsville, Dallas, Fort Worth, Galveston/Houston, and San Antonio.

"In some parts of our nation, you're trying to resurrect the faith. Here, you're just trying to keep up with how fast it's growing," Bishop Kevin Farrell of Dallas said in 2008.

Here's a vignette from America's new Catholic frontier:

If you're not careful, attempts to describe the congregation at Good Shepherd Catholic Church in tiny Johnson City, Texas, can sound like a routine from a stand-up comedian: "A white rancher, a Mexican day laborer, and a Nigerian prince walk into a parish." All that's required is changing "parish" to "bar," and you've got a setup in search of a punch line. This is no joke, however, but the social reality in Johnson City, population 1,500 on a good day.

The small parish of 70 families has traditionally been mostly white—or, in the argot of the southwest, "Anglo"—descendants of European Catholics who settled in Texas after its 1836 declaration of independence from Mexico. The parish also draws a few *Tejanos*, meaning Hispanics who have lived in Texas for generations, in some cases since the Spanish colonial era. (The unofficial *Tejano* motto is, "We didn't cross the border; the border crossed us.") There's a small but growing number of recent immigrants from Mexico, often drawn to work on ranches or in service industries.

The improbable pastor of this Tex/Mex mix is Fr. Nichodemus Ejimabo, an Ibo tribesman from Orlu state in eastern Nigeria. The mere presence of a Nigerian in rural Texas would, perhaps, be noteworthy enough, but Ejimabo is no ordinary Nigerian. Back home, his father is a village chief, making Ejimabo an Ibo prince. He's also a former striker on the Nigerian national soccer team, the "Super Eagles." Johnson City thus offers a metaphor for today's American Church, where dramatic population growth and accelerating cultural diversity are shaping the new face—or, perhaps more accurately, a whole series of new faces—of Catholicism.

What Does This Transformation Mean?

For one thing, it will inevitably mean a Church more in touch with the plight of the poor, especially immigrants, as Catholics scramble to care for new arrivals who are often poor, abused, and exploited, and sometimes caught in a Kafka-esque maze of shifting and seemingly arbitrary immigration policies.

To watch the Church in action at that level, one has only to drop in at Casa Juan Diego on Houston's west side. It's a sprawling welcome center for immigrants that includes shelters for men, women, and children, food and clothing banks (distributing between 10 and 15 tons of food every week), a health clinic (including dental services), and residences for sick and disabled, all operated under the umbrella of the Catholic Worker movement. Casa Juan Diego was founded by Mark and Louise Zwick, who spent a brief period in El Salvador during its bloody civil war in the 1970s. They created Casa Juan Diego to care for refugees fleeing violence in Central America, but today find themselves working with vast numbers of new immigrants, most from Mexico.

Among other services, Casa Juan Diego operates a residence for 15 sick and disabled people and pays $500 to $1,000 a month for long-term care for roughly 70 other people. In many cases, Louise Zwick said, these are undocumented immigrants who took high-risk, low-pay jobs to support themselves and their families, such as working on scaffolds on construction sites. If they get hurt, she said, they're basically on their own.

"Every day, we get a call from a hospital social worker saying we have this person who has no family to take care of him,"

Mark Zwick said. "He's a paraplegic, or he's paralyzed, or he just needs a few months to get on his feet. There's no government support, there's no disability, no Medicaid, nothing. We take care of him."

The engaged, activist spirit will mark many of the most promising currents in American Catholicism in the century to come.

The new demographic profile of Catholicism in America will also likely mean a Church less caught up in polarizing internal debates over issues such as papal authority or the fine points of liturgical practice. Fr. Robert Williams, pastor of Good Shepherd parish in a largely Hispanic region of Dallas, says that he actually stopped reading most national Catholic publications several years ago, because the issues that loom largest in their pages simply don't have anything to do with his pastoral realities.

These currents seem to be handing the

Church in the United States a golden opportunity to become a model of what a truly multi-cultural, multi-lingual, polychrome family of faith looks like, and how it can celebrate that diversity without being fractured by it. American Catholicism has the historical opportunity to become an exemplar of how Houston's Cardinal Daniel Di Nardo describes life in his archdiocese: "Happy chaos."

When hope runs low, there's nothing like the prospect of a transcendent cause to help people set aside their angst and to embrace new possibilities. That, in a nutshell, is precisely the situation of American Catholicism at the dawn of the twenty-first century.

A New Generation

Looking at the next generation of Catholic leaders in the United States—meaning the rising cohort of twenty-something priests, religious, and lay activists—some analysts fear a kind of turning inward for the American Church, even a return to a Catholic ghetto, because these young Catholics seem considerably more "conservative." Empirical data confirming that impression are certainly not difficult to find.

Consider, for example, a study released in August by the Center for Applied Research in the Apostolate at Georgetown University, which was carried out on behalf of the National Religious Vocations Conference, of trends in vocations to religious life in the United States. With regard to theological and spiritual outlooks, the CARA study found clear differences between the "Millennial Generation," meaning religious born after 1982, and the "Vatican II Generation," meaning religious men and women born between 1943 and 1960. Millennials are far more likely to say they entered religious life out of a desire for commitment to the Church, and that they entered their specific community because of its reputation for fidelity to the Church. They're more likely to wear habits, more likely to say that devotions such as eucharistic adoration and the Liturgy of the Hours are "very important," less eager to do ministry in non-Catholic or non-confessional settings, and more positive in their attitudes about authority.

The obvious corollary is that religious orders which foster a more traditional ethos tend to have better luck attracting younger members. One clear sign of which way the winds are blowing: Just one per-

cent of women's communities belonging
to the Leadership Conference of Women
Religious, known for having a more liberal
outlook, currently have more than ten new
members in initial formation, whereas a
robust 28 percent of communities belonging to the Conference of Major Superiors of
Women, known for being more conservative, have ten or more members in the early
stages of membership.

Yet to hastily affix the label "conservative" upon this new generation is poten-
tially misleading. It assumes an ideological
frame of reference, when in fact the situation might more profitably be understood
in terms of historical dynamics.

Simply put, the generation currently
running the show in the Church, whether in
the bishops' conference or in the theological
guild, was perhaps the last to come of age in
a homogenously Catholic environment, the
Catholic "ghetto" of American lore, which

one either embraced or chafed against; but in any event, the primary cultural influence was the Church. Today's generation didn't grow up in that world. The primary social milieu in which they came of age wasn't shaped by the Church but rather by secular anomie and American pop culture. Their hunger for identity and their lack of a chip on the shoulder about ecclesiastical authority isn't so much about choosing one side or another in the Church's debates as it is about reacting to (and, in some cases, against) the values and lifestyles the broader society has offered them.

Proof of the point comes when you drill down a bit with these younger Catholics, inquiring about their attitudes and values across a wide range of matters. What you will often find is that these allegedly "conservative" young believers, the very same people who queue up in long lines at the confessional and who openly profess their admiration for Pope Benedict XVI, also quite often have a striking ecological sensitivity, a deep desire to serve the poor, and are sharply critical of both the death penalty and armed conflict.

All that points to a deeply intriguing possibility: The tendency of American Catholics to splinter into left and right, to forever emphasize one aspect of the Church's social message at the expense of another, may be tied to a particular generation's experience. There is, therefore, reason to hope that a new generation may bring with it a fresh perspective.

Of course, the tensions inside the Catholic Church between left and right, between those inclined to emphasize tradition and those seeking détente with the modern world, are not simply going to dissolve. A defining challenge for twenty-first century Catholicism will be the capacity to do two things simultaneously: to foster a strong

sense of traditional Catholic identity, en-
suring that we do not, in Jacques Maritain's
memorable phrase, end up kneeling before
the world; and at the same time not to close
in upon ourselves, but to harness the best of
all the various Catholic temperaments and
instincts in order to get on with the busi-
ness of transforming the world in light of
the Gospel.

In many ways, the coming generation of
Catholics seems ideally positioned to take
up that challenge. They are the sons and
daughters of the secular world, fully aware
of both its lights and its shadows, and at the
same time they are eager to embrace a full-
bodied ethos of Catholic distinctiveness.
That can be an enormously positive force
for the Church in America, if that force is
not artificially diverted and redirected. To
put this point as bluntly as possible, the old-
er generation of Catholic liberals will need
to resist feeling threatened by this new co-

hort, and Catholic conservatives will need to resist the urge to look at younger Catholics and claim victory.

When one removes the blinders sometimes imposed by ideological prejudice, what the new generation actually seems to augur is not a victory for one side or the other in the Church's internal contests. Rather, the rise of this new generation seems to signify that the whole game is changing.

Conclusion

In the brilliant (and, by the way, richly Christological) movie, *The Shawshank Redemption*, Tim Robbins plays a young banker named Andy Dufresne who's unjustly convicted of murdering his wife and shipped off to the notorious Shawshank Prison. At one stage, Dufresne is tossed into solitary confinement after he locks the warden's office and plays a hauntingly beautiful aria from Mozart's opera, *Le Nozze di Figaro,* over the prison loudspeakers. Sitting at a lunch table with his fellow convicts after he finally gets out, he explains that he survived solitary by carrying the memory of the music into the hole.

Dufresne's best friend in Shawshank, the wise prison veteran, Red, played by Morgan Freeman, warns Andy against spreading too many positive vibes. Hope, Red says, is a dangerous thing in a place like Shawshank.

"Hope is a good thing, maybe the best of things," Dufresne replies, "and no good thing ever dies."

Without a doubt, American Catholics can be forgiven for feeling sometimes like they've been tossed into the hole at Shawshank. Our Church often seems divided and demoralized, traumatized by scandal, and we can occasionally seem bereft of visionary leadership. The Church in the United States can appear, in the title of one influential recent book, to be "a people adrift."

Yet the truth is that it has always been thus in the Catholic Church. There never was a golden age in which there was no basis for disillusionment or heartache; as the quip goes, the "good old days" were formerly known as "these trying times." The Catholic Church is an infinitely complex reality whose footprint extends through time and across space, and as a result, there will always be something to lament and something to celebrate, usually in roughly equal measure.

The glass, in other words, will always be half full and half empty.

As a community with a vocation to hope, the trick is to confront the crises we will always face without losing sight of the positive energy that's also coursing through the Church. As we've seen, the early twenty-first century is rich with the raw material for hope, both around the Catholic world and right here in the United States. The challenge is to convert those resources into accomplishment.

About the Author

John L. Allen, Jr., is the senior correspondent for the *National Catholic Reporter* and senior Vatican analyst for CNN. He's also the author of *The Rise of Benedict XVI* (Doubleday, 2005), *The Future Church: How Ten Trends are Revolutionizing the Catholic Church* (Doubleday, 2009), and *10 Things Pope Benedict Wants You to Know* (Liguori Publications, 2007).